Peace and Calm

THE LITTLE BOOK ON GRIEF
Concerns to Consider
By
Iris and Kit

"These days are the winter of the soul,
But spring comes and brings new life
and beauty
Because of the growth of the roots
in the dark"

"Aunt Jill"
(Sarah B. Reeves)

Part One

––––– ❧ ⟪◈⟫ ☙ –––––

Introduction

Foreword

The pain and mourning process associated with the loss of a loved one, at its core, is the affirmation that we have loved.

Iris Bolton and Kit Casey, authors of "the Little Book on Grief," share their personal insights and considerations based on their experiences dealing with many common aspects of grief. Their thoughtful words, formulated from their own loss of a loved one, provide practical antidotes for many of the emotions and experiences encountered during the mourning process. While everyone's journey is unique, the essence of healing is grounded in hope, assurance that we are normal and having the right tools to take care of ourselves.

During your healing journey, know that you are not alone. Often reaching out to family and friends or clergy to talk it out can help you see things more clearly and, most importantly, acknowledge your feelings.

Each person's road to recovery is distinctive and unlike any other. Looking back at my personal experiences, each path to healing was different with every loss. I would often go back and forth between the various phases or "stages" of grief, sometimes facing more than one at a time, or skipping a phase altogether. It's important to know there is no right or wrong way to grieve.

You may feel or experience everything listed on the pages that follow or only a few. Find those considerations that connect with you and make this guide to healing and recovery your own.

Bill Bolton
Iris and Jack Bolton's son

I Don't Know Why

by Iris

I don't know why.
I'll never know why.
I don't have to know why. I don't like it.
I don't have to like it.
What I do have to do is make a choice
about my living.
What I do want to do is accept it and go
on living.
The choice is mine.
I can go on living,
Valuing every moment in a way I never
did before
Or I can be destroyed by it and, in turn,
destroy others.
I thought I was immortal,
That my family and my children were
also.
That tragedy happened only to others.
But I know now that life is tenuous and
valuable.
So I am choosing to go on living,
making the
Most of the time I have, valuing my
family and
Friends in a way never possible before.

7

How to use
THE LITTLE BOOK ON GRIEF
Concerns and Considerations

This book is divided into six parts:

1. Introduction
2. What You May Be Feeling After the Death of a Loved One: Concerns and Considerations
3. What You May Be Experiencing After the Death of a Loved One: Concerns and Considerations
4. Self-Care Suggestions: Concerns and Considerations
5. Finding Support Suggestions
6. Acknowledgments

The Index in the back of the book gives easy access to different issues such as guilt, anger, fear and confusion. You'll find one "concern" on each page, with suggestions for coping called "Consider this."

This little book is not intended as advice, therapy or even deep thinking about grief. Its purpose is to share practical wisdom given birth through the pain and sorrow of both authors.

Every painting created by Kit Casey is a sacred rendering of emotions representing each section of the book. Open yourself to the holy flow, the extraordinary outpouring from her subconscious, as the colors spill across each page.

All matter has energy and this little book has a kind of magical energy all its own.

Readers have said, "Just by holding a copy of the book, I feel comforted."

Another shared, "I feel a subtle vibration. The energy of compassion and love seems to be imprinted on every page and painting."

LETTER FROM THE AUTHORS:
Iris and Kit

Dear Friend,

Welcome to "The Little Book on Grief."
We are grateful it has found its way into
your hands. If you, or someone you know,
have experienced the death of a loved one,
this may be the moment of discovering the
support you need. The purpose of this little
book is to provide comfort and focused,
practical guidance.

First, we offer our condolences. We are
deeply sorry for your loss. Both of us have
had our own struggles in managing the
death of loved ones, with feelings and
experiences of grief that may be similar to
yours. We don't have answers. We do have
thoughts for you to consider, and a few
suggestions based on our own losses.

Following the death of a loved one, a sacred
process develops which is known as "grief,"

"mourning" or "medicine for the soul" to heal your loss. It is not a single event. It is a process, or journey, that takes time. The anguish can be so debilitating that you may desire simplified, compassionate direction from other wounded hearts.

Life somehow never prepares us for death. Whether sudden or anticipated, the death of a loved one is visceral, consuming and alarmingly final. We all mourn differently, and comparison to others is rarely of service.

A natural response to death or loss, grief for most people is exhausting and expressive of a series of painful feelings that overwhelm and repeat. Given time and the deliberate facing of all aspects of grief (guilt, anger, sadness, etc.), your angst can be calmed. This allows you to gradually move forward into your forever-changed, reframed life.

In this book we have listed issues or "concerns" which may surface during your mourning. You may only relate to some of them. Take what is useful. We trust you will relate to our stories, and in time, you may allow the force of your experience to help others.

Warm personal regards,

Chris and Kit

Table of Contents

Part Two

——◆❧❦❧◆——

What You May Be Feeling

Turmoil and Sorrow

16

"We long to avoid this fierce, yet holy pilgrimage. Yet grief, as painful a season as it is, is a necessary part of our healing. To run from grief is to run from the very thing that can quell the pain of our loss."

William Cowper
18th Century English Poet

BASIC TRUTHS TO REMEMBER
After the Death of a Loved One

Grief is confusing, complicated and different for everyone. As you face this healing journey, let us remind you of some basic truths. As touchstones, may they give you strength and courage to heal your heart.

1. *Resilience:*
   The human spirit is resilient. Emotional healing is exhausting, yet possible.

2. *Hope:*
   There is always hope, even when you feel hopeless.

3. *Patience:*
   It is important to be patient with yourself while grieving because you are experiencing many strong emotions all at once. Time is your friend.

4. *Courage:*
   It takes bravery and courage to survive the death of a loved one.

5. *Faith / Spirituality:*
   Your faith or spirituality may bring you strength and comfort. A state of grace surrounds you like a warm blanket as you grieve.

6. *Gratitude:*
   Even in death there are things for which you can be grateful, ("She isn't suffering any more," or "I was able to love him for ten years.")

7. *Help:*
   Asking for help is a strong and positive option, and necessary for most of us.

8. *Knowledge:*
   What you do know for certain has not changed (love for your children, love of sun on your face or a warm chocolate chip cookie, etc.).

9. *Emotions:*
    Children are taught that there are four
    basic emotions: mad, sad, glad and
    scared. This simplification helps identify
    your feelings, so they can be expressed
    appropriately.

10. *Change:*
    Change is not comfortable yet is to be
    expected as a part of life. It is impossible
    to prepare for such transitions and it can
    feel scary.

WHAT YOU MAY BE FEELING
After the Death of a Loved One
Concerns and Considerations

After the death of a loved one, emotions may tumble around in your heart with a force unknown to you. You may have feelings that are confusing. You may have NO feelings, as the shock creates numbness or disconnection. You may feel as though you are losing your mind as you ride an emotional roller coaster. You are not! You are in grief. The following is a list of what you might be feeling. We hope this will help clarify and normalize the chaos within you.

1. The shock of the death
2. Why?
3. Guilt
4. Anger
5. Rage
6. Stress
7. Anxiety
8. Overwhelm
9. Sadness
10. Depression / Hopelessness

11. Emotional roller coaster
12. PTSD (post-traumatic stress syndrome)
13. Blame
14. Pain (emotional / physical)
15. Loneliness / Isolation
16. Fear
17. Loss of identity and purpose
18. Shame
19. Meltdown
20. Feeling like a burden
21. Feeling "crazy"
22. Failure
23. Relief
24. Envy
25. Control
26. Faith / Spirituality
27. Vulnerability

WHAT YOU MAY BE FEELING
Concerns and Considerations

1. **The Concern... The shock of the death**
   You can't believe it. You are in shock!

   Consider this...
   It is hard to believe that your loved one is gone. You are stunned. It is unbelievable to you, even if it was expected. It is natural to deny (the phone rings and you think your loved one is calling you). Love yourself through this time.

   Put one foot in front of the other. Eat and sleep when you feel like it. Each new day brings strength for that day. Give yourself time to accept the truth. Give yourself time.

2. The Concern...Why?

Why did this have to happen? Why now? Why me?

Consider this...

"Why?" is the eternal question. Why did he have to die? Why couldn't I have saved her? Ask whatever questions you need to ask until you find some answers or hunches you can live with. Keep asking until you find some peace.

3. **The Concern...Guilt**
   It is common to blame yourself for your loved one's death.

   Consider this...
   You may feel guilty about something you did or didn't do for the person who died, and even blame yourself for their death. We all do the best we can with who we are and what we know at the time, taking into account our strengths and weaknesses.

   Choosing to forgive yourself will ease your pain. In time, the destructiveness of guilt may turn to regret, which is more like disappointment, and easier to carry.

4. **The Concern... Anger**
   I am so angry at my loved one for
   leaving me. I am angry at God and at
   everything.

   Consider this...
   It is not fair and you have a right to be
   angry. Feel what you need to feel. Try
   to allow it without judging yourself.
   Underneath the anger is usually hurt,
   and you have been deeply wounded.

5. **The Concern...Rage**
   When anger builds up and gets out of
   control, it may become rage.

   Consider this...
   Anger can become destructive, if
   denied. Find an outlet for your anger
   before it turns into rage. You can
   exercise, express your creativity or talk
   to someone you trust. Professional help
   is always an option.

6. **The Concern…Stress**
    Due to the death of your loved one and
    the ongoing demands of daily life, you
    may feel stressed out.

    Consider this…
    Stress can be manageable. Make a "to
    do" list. Check off items one at a time.
    Ask for help and delegate so you have
    less on your plate; then go back to bed
    or put your feet up. You don't have to
    be superwoman or superman.

    Go slowly and do one thing at a time.
    Simplify!

7. **The Concern... Anxiety**
   Stress and worry are amplified in grief and may lead to anxiety. Getting through the day may seem impossible.

   Consider this...
   You are suffering the loss of your loved one, yet you are expected to function and carry on, even with the weight of emotions you bear. Be gentle and patient with yourself. Tell someone about your anxiety, including your doctor.

   Sharing your worry, fear and hurt can lessen its power over you. Take your grief one day at a time, one issue at a time, one emotion at a time. Help from a professional can quiet your anxiety.

8. **The Concern…Overwhelm**
    Overwhelm is caused by complicated
    emotional and physical responses to the
    death of a loved one. Multiple feelings
    and demands rush at you with the pain
    grief brings. It can be debilitating.

    Consider this…
    Your world has changed now. You
    may be overloaded and overwhelmed
    with powerful feelings and heavy
    responsibilities. You may need to just
    stop. Take a nap.

    Take time out mentally and physically,
    without guilt. This is a time to take care
    of you. This is a time to ask for help.

9. **The Concern...Sadness**

Loss and death create sorrow, disappointment, and sadness. Your loved one is no longer here, and you miss them.

Consider this...

Sadness can be a constant companion or it can alternate with the other emotions of grief, washing over you when you least expect it. This can occur when you simply miss their company or when you see or hear something that reminds you of him or her. Its depth depends on your relationship with the person who died.

In time, sadness can change, become less frequent and shift to gratitude for your loved one having been in your life at all.

10. The Concern…Depression /
Hopelessness

During the process of mourning, it is common to feel depressed and hopeless. You may feel that you have no power to move on and that your depression will never leave you.

Consider this…
You are deeply sad because of a specific event, the death of your loved one. Depression, however, is a general sadness that you can't put your finger on, that seeps into all areas of your life. It can rob you of your appetite, your energy, and your joy for living. It can leave you hopeless.

If you feel your sadness has turned to depression, ask for help. You do not have to travel this road alone; you do not have to live with depression.

If you feel like joining your loved one in death, or feel suicidal, please tell someone and call a counselor now.

Thinking about ending your life does not mean you will act on those thoughts. It means you are in unbearable pain and may need help.

11. **The Concern...Emotional roller coaster**
    Your feelings can go from high to low in
    what feels like a minute.

    Consider this...
    You can be devastated one second
    and hopeful the next. Most people
    experience this up and down of
    emotions. It can be exhausting but
    will calm with time. Allow it without
    judgment.

12. **The Concern…PTSD (post-traumatic stress disorder)**

    PTSD is defined in the professional's DSM-5, the diagnostic and statistical manual, as "A mental condition that involves a recurring memory that is caused by directly or indirectly witnessing or experiencing a horrific event. Individuals suffering with PTSD have intense, disturbing thoughts and feelings related to the traumatic experience that lasts long after the initial occurrence of the traumatic event."

    Consider this…

    We consulted with Atlanta psychotherapist, Elaine Gibson, LPC, LMFT, with fifty years of experience. She said, "Have compassion for your humanness. PTSD is a common response to profound trauma. It is important to acknowledge the event so that you can eventually accept the truth of what happened. This allows you to move forward.

Facing the horror and flashbacks are the beginning of the healing. It means you are courageous enough to see the truth and face it. Consider getting professional help for this concern. Remember that asking for help is a sign of strength in this circumstance."

13. **The Concern...Blame**
Blame can be a knee jerk reaction to tragedy and grief. You want to blame someone or something for your loss and your pain.

Consider this...
In grief, pointing a finger at yourself or others is the attempt to make sense of what has happened. You want to know whose fault it is. Blame is a natural response yet wastes energy. You may have to deal with others blaming you for not doing enough before the death. They may blame you for making different choices than they wanted. That is their problem. Try not to let it become yours.

You can learn to agree to disagree. Eventually, there can be forgiveness for yourself and for others.

14. **The Concern…Pain (emotional/physical)**

You may feel broken emotionally which can lead to actual physical pain.

Consider this…

Emotional pain and heartache can lead to actual physical pain. It can feel like your heart is broken open, which may lead to painful physical symptoms. Physical pain can mend in time, yet the heartbreak may feel like a wound that takes longer to heal. Both will lessen and become softer as you process your grief.

15. **The Concern...Loneliness / Isolation**
    Loneliness is a feeling that you are alone
    and disconnected from others.

    Consider this...
    You may actually be alone with little
    support or you may just be feeling
    lonely. You may believe that nobody
    understands your pain, so you might be
    isolating yourself. There is a difference
    between being alone and being lonely.

    Grieving by yourself some of the time
    is important, but shutting yourself off
    from others amplifies your grief and
    your loneliness. Look for the balance
    between the two.

16. **The Concern...Fear**

Fear can be overwhelming after someone dies. You might wonder: "What will happen to me now? ...to my family? Who else will die? I see everything through the eyes of fear. I'm afraid this pain will never leave me. How can I go on living without my loved one?"

Consider this...

Fear of the change this death will bring is natural; the unknown and the unexpected can be scary. Look at what is legitimate fear and what is unrealistic or unfounded. Express your fears to a wise friend or to a counselor.

Let your faith and trust in life calm your fears with compassion for yourself. Most fears do not become a reality.

17. **The Concern…Loss of identity and purpose**
Since the death of my beloved one, I don't know who I am. What is my role now and what is my purpose in life?

Consider this…
You are experiencing a time of change, uncertainty and confusion. Your world makes no sense and seems upside-down. You may have lost your role as caretaker, wife, friend, parent, etc. and perhaps your purpose in life, for now.

Change *is* happening, but remember that your identity and character, with the tools and strength to carry on, are still intact. In time, your world, and your role in it, will make sense again.

18. **The Concern... Shame**

Shame is connected to cultural beliefs set by the community. When cultural and moral standards are defied, there may be a sense that you have done something wrong. You may have a feeling of transgression, inadequacy or embarrassment, especially when a suicide is involved.

Consider this...

Shame is a waste of energy brought on by fear, not love. Your standards need to be set by you, not the community, so allow yourself freedom from the stigma. You may have to educate others about changing beliefs. For example, cancer was once considered shameful. Today people understand it is a disease with no shame. Cancer can be devastating, yet no cause for shame.

19. **The Concern...Meltdowns**

Meltdowns are caused by the buildup of emotions to the point that an emotional explosion is almost inevitable.

Consider this...
Sobbing, an emotional outbreak, and feeling out of control are all signs of pent-up emotions that need release. They are like a balloon filled with air to the breaking point. Though you may consider it a weakness, a meltdown can be therapeutic, an outpouring of all the intense emotions built up by grief.

Allow the meltdown and redefine it as letting go.

20. **The Concern...Feeling like a burden**
    When you think you are causing
    someone worry and adding to their
    responsibilities, you may feel like a
    burden.

    Consider this...
    In truth, sharing your grief lessens its
    emotional grip on everyone involved.
    There is strength in pain shared,
    compassion and relief in talking things
    through. Recognize that if someone is
    worried about you, it is a reflection of
    their love.

    The gift of learning to give and receive
    is priceless.

21. **The Concern...Feeling "crazy"**
    In grief, you can feel like you are losing
    your mind.

    Consider this...
    The truth is that you are not crazy. You
    may *feel* like you are losing your mind.
    You are not; you are in mourning.
    Confusion and loss of memory are
    common. Losing a loved one, no matter
    how they died, is traumatic. Be patient
    with yourself.

22. **The Concern... Failure**

A sense of failure can develop if you
believe you failed to keep your loved
one alive.

Consider this...

You may have the belief that if love is
strong enough, it can save a life and that
if you had done more, they might still
be alive. It is *not* within your power
to keep someone alive. Many forces
contribute. Accept the fact of their
death. Understand that you did all that
you could.

23. The Concern...Relief

If your loved one had been suffering, there may be a sense of relief after their death.

Consider this...
Relief is a loving response to their death. Guilt may surface if you believe you should not feel this way. Consider that you love the person enough to accept the relief that comes with the end of their suffering.

24. **The Concern…Envy**
Feelings of jealousy may surface when you are overwhelmed with grief and you see that others are apparently happy.

Consider this…
Know that envy is a common aspect of grief because others may look like they are not suffering as you are. It feels as if the world should stop because of your loss. Be careful not to judge yourself or others. You never know what they are dealing with in the moment. Envy is often temporary.

25. The Concern...Control

After someone dies you may feel powerless.

Consider this...

You may feel like you have control over nothing. You may feel powerless and helpless. The truth is that you do have control over yourself, your responses, and asking for what you need.

26. **The Concern...Faith / Spirituality**
    After someone dies, your faith may
    bring you comfort, or it may leave you
    angry and confused.

    Consider this...
    For some people, faith brings peace
    and trust. For others, anger and
    blame may surface and shake their
    beliefs. Talking to friends and family
    members who have experienced loss
    and faith challenges may provide
    some understanding. Speaking with a
    compassionate member of the clergy
    may also help. As an alternative to
    a religious faith, reliance on your
    own unique spirituality may provide
    comfort.

27. The Concern...Vulnerability

Most people feel vulnerable and super-sensitive after the death of their loved one.

Consider this...

Keep in mind that you are emotionally raw during grief. Self-care is critical at this time. If you hear words that are hurtful or wounding, walk away or find ways to protect yourself. Consider talking to someone about the criticisms, so they don't build up and become magnified. In time, you will be less vulnerable and more at peace.

Part Three

———————✦✧❀✦✧———————

What You May Be Experiencing

Chaos and Grief

"What we once enjoyed and deeply loved
we can never lose, for all that we love
deeply becomes part of us."

Helen Keller

WHAT YOU MAY BE EXPERIENCING
After the Death of a Loved One
Concerns and Considerations

The death of a loved one may be a new experience for you. There can be many unknowns and surprising events. The list below identifies some of these. To name them helps you know you are not alone, and that your experience is common to others as well.

1. Morning awakening
2. Unresolved conflict with the deceased
3. Advice
4. Change in relationships with friends and family
5. Invitations
6. Funerals
7. Multiple deaths
8. Remnants of a prior loss
9. Responsibilities
10. Job return
11. Parenting while grieving
12. Photographs
13. Belongings

14. Gossip / Rumors
15. Grieving differently
16. Timetable for grief
17. Secrets
18. Curiosity seekers
19. Cultural differences / Diversity
20. Protecting / Defending your loved one's image
21. Firsts: Anniversary / Birthday / Holiday
22. Triggers
23. Tears
24. Moving
25. Purpose and meaning in life

WHAT YOU MAY BE EXPERIENCING
Concerns and Considerations

1. **The Concern...Morning awakening**
   Getting out of bed in the morning may
   seem impossible.

   Consider this...
   You are waking up to your grief and
   sorrow. It can be overwhelming. Start by
   taking a few deep breaths. Stretch and
   drink a glass of water. Be gentle with
   yourself. Do one thing at a time and you
   will get through this day.

2. **The Concern…Unresolved conflict with the deceased**
    Prior conflict can make grieving complicated and even more painful.

    Consider this…
    If your loved one dies with conflict present in your relationship, powerful emotions such as anger, blame and disappointment may surface. These unresolved feelings have no impact on them and hurt you alone, even preventing your own healing.

    Learning to let go and forgive yourself and the deceased is the key to resolution. This can be done by letting your feelings out: writing them out, painting them out, exercising them out, talking them out. This, with time, makes it possible to reach a place of peace and understanding with your loved one.

3. **The Concern... Advice**
   In an effort to be helpful, people will tell
   you what to do.

   Consider this...
   If you find you are getting an overload
   of well-intended advice, you may want
   to set limits and boundaries with others.
   You could say, "Thank you for your
   suggestion. I will think about that."

4. **The Concern…Change in relationships with friends and family**
   After a death, relationships may change. Some positively, some negatively.

   Consider this…
   Some people around you may be very helpful, some overly helpful, and others not at all. It can be hard for even the best-intentioned of friends to know how to respond. Some may disappear, not being able to understand your pain. Death affects everyone differently.

   Speak up for yourself, and tell people what you need and what you don't need.

5. **The Concern...Invitations**
   Social invitations may come too soon for
   you and feel like a burden.

   Consider this...
   Friends want to distract you from
   your pain and may invite you to lunch
   or gatherings outside the house. If
   anything does not feel right, take care of
   yourself and communicate clearly. You
   can say, "Thank you for asking. I just
   can't do that right now."

6. **The Concern…Funerals**
   If a traditional funeral is not held, or
   your attendance is not possible, the
   healing process may be delayed.

   Consider this…
   Most people need the ceremony of a
   funeral to say goodbye to their loved
   one. If for some reason you cannot
   attend a scheduled service, you can plan
   to be there in spirit. When no funeral
   is possible, like during the pandemic,
   consider doing a ceremony online with
   friends and family.

   When the time is right, make a plan that
   takes care of your needs and offers you
   some peace.

7. **The Concern... Multiple deaths**
   Multiple deaths at the same time may
   compound the emotional impact, as well
   as your pain. It is hard to grieve more
   than one person at a time.

   Consider this...
   Depending upon the relationship you
   had with each person, you may not grieve
   them equally, or you may experience
   guilt about one, while feeling anger about
   another. That is okay. Allow the grief
   process to happen naturally, as thoughts
   come up about each loved one.

   Grieving one person more than the other
   does not mean there is less love. You may
   need some professional help with this
   difficult situation.

8. **The Concern…Remnants of a prior loss**
   Death of a loved one can reopen long-standing feelings of loss.

   Consider this…
   A recent death may re-awaken the heartache of a death that occurred years ago. Though painful to be reminded of a previous loss, it may demonstrate to you the strength, courage and coping skills you had then that got you through.

   Remnants of grief, or grief still in process, can become an opportunity to soothe those old wounds.

9. **The Concern...Responsibilities**
Paperwork and finances await your attention. The thought of them is overwhelming and you want to ignore them.

Consider this...
Delegate! Ask for help. Is there someone you can trust to assist you? Speak to a financial advisor or lawyer. See if you can focus on doing one thing a day, such as paying a bill. Eventually you can build a habit--tend to business one step at a time--until life's demands become manageable.

10. **The Concern...Job return**

The time to return to work is different for everyone.

Consider this...

Many businesses offer one week of bereavement leave. The grieving process takes much longer. There are numerous and understandable reasons why some people return to work as suggested by the workplace. There is no right or wrong here. If one week is not enough time for you to get back on your feet, negotiate for more.

Trust your instincts; do what feels right and is manageable for you.

11. **The Concern…Parenting while grieving**
Grief can be all-consuming which can make parenting more difficult and debilitating.

Consider this…
Ask for help during this time so you have breaks to be alone and grieve quietly. Depending upon the age of your children, they can help you through your sadness in different ways. If they are young, their cheery energy is comforting, and a reminder of our unconditional love for one another. If they are older, special bonds and appreciation can develop as you listen and share your feelings and perceptions of loss, death and dying.

12. **The Concern...Photographs**
    Displaying photos of your loved one or removing them can be a dilemma.

    Consider this...
    Leaving photos displayed may be of comfort to some, while for others they act as a constant reminder of their loss. Ask for what you want. If family members living in your home have different needs and responses, consider a compromise that removes the photographs from shared spaces and allows them in private ones. This could support everyone.

13. The Concern…Belongings

Sorting your loved one's clothes and belongings into "keep" or "giveaway" can be exhausting and heart wrenching.

Consider this…
Sort your loved one's things at your own pace. It does not have to be done immediately. For some people, having their loved one's belongings around brings pain. Acting quickly helps with closure. For others, keeping familiar belongings in the space can ease the process and pain of letting go.

Just do what feels right for you, and in your own time. It may help you to ask for assistance, or you may want to do it alone. You can always store things to work on later when you are feeling stronger.

14. The Concern…Gossip / Rumors

A strange reaction for a few people is to gossip or spread rumors, especially if the death is by suicide. Be aware that this can happen.

Consider this…

Some people love drama, and sometimes they will change the facts for the effect it has. When you ignore gossip, its power is removed. However, if you feel the need to defend, clarify the facts. Speak the truth.

15. **The Concern...Grieving differently**
    No two people grieve in the same way.

    Consider this...
    There is no right or wrong way to
    grieve. Everyone grieves differently.
    Others may tell you how to grieve or
    how long your grief should last. Stay
    true to yourself. The process is very
    personal. It takes longer than expected
    and can be an exhausting process.

16. **The Concern…Timetable for grief**
    You may feel pressure from yourself
    and others to "get over" your loss and
    return to "normal."

    Consider this…
    A common question for mourners is
    "Will my grief ever end? Will I ever
    get over this death and get back to my
    old self?" Don't pressure yourself to
    "get over it." Grieve in your own way
    and for as long as you need. The truth
    is, there is no getting over the loss of a
    loved one. Instead, you assimilate it into
    your life and gradually move forward
    emotionally and physically.

    By placing one foot in front of the other,
    one day at a time, you learn to live
    without them.

17. **The Concern...Secrets**
    There may be secrets about how the
    person died, especially if it was by
    suicide.

    Consider this...
    Secrets may be kept to protect someone,
    especially if the death was by suicide.
    The lie can be more harmful than the
    truth. Consider not keeping secrets.
    They may backfire and become a burden
    to maintain, and actually increase the
    pain of your mourning.

18. **The Concern...Curiosity seekers**
    Some people are curious and pushy to
    know every detail of your loved one's
    death.

    Consider this...
    Steer clear of these people. You can
    share as much or as little as you choose.
    Know that you do not need to be
    coerced into saying anything that makes
    you uncomfortable.

19. **The Concern...Cultural differences /
Diversity**
"Diversity is the range of human
differences," says Webster's Dictionary.
Sometimes there can be conflict about
the funeral, burial traditions or even the
grief process within the family.

Consider this...
Response to death varies widely within
different cultures and traditions.
Seek to honor the different customs
and accommodate each other with no
judgment. You may not like it, but this is
where your negotiation skills can shine.

20. **The Concern…Protecting / Defending your loved one's image**

Some people may remember your loved one as being quite different from your reality. You may want to defend a derogatory comment or share your point of view when the person is remembered as "perfect."

Consider this…

The "perfect" or the "flawed" person they remember may be fictional. Listening to their perspective without judgment can be difficult yet may keep peace. Allow others to maintain their image of the person without challenge, if you can. However, if you are compelled to speak your truth, be prepared for losing the relationship. Ask yourself if it is worth it.

21. **The Concern...Firsts: Anniversary /
Birthday / Holiday**
The first few years of any special day
without your loved one is extremely
difficult.

Consider this...
You may dread these special days.
For some, the anticipation leading up
to them may be more emotional and
depleting than the actual day itself.
Memories of important days, either sad
or joyful, may bubble up and feel like
they just happened yesterday. A kind
of time warp may occur. Try to have a
game plan.

Do what feels right to you. Others who
are grieving may feel a need "to do
something" in honor of their loved one.
You don't have to join in unless you
want to do so. You could start a new
tradition.

I, Iris, can tell you that after my son's death, I wanted to honor him on remembrance days, such as his birthday or the anniversary of his passing. I now will introduce myself to strangers (usually a mother and child) and explain that I wish to give them a gift in honor of my son who died. As I hand them my cash offering, I ask that they simply accept in the spirit in which it is given.

The amount is not important, yet the gift usually brings a thank you, a hug and often tears. It is always a joy to do and becomes a fun day instead of a downer. Now I look forward to those "give away" days.

22. The Concern...Triggers

A "trigger" can happen at any time and anywhere. It may be something such as a fragrance, a song, or anything in your environment reminiscent of your loved one.

Consider this...

There may be days when you are feeling healthier and more hopeful, when suddenly something reminds you of your loss. A phone call from someone unaware of your loved one's passing can cause a wave of grief to wash over you. These triggers are to be expected and they are exhausting.

You can be slammed with the reality of your loss and caught off guard. These upsets *do* quiet over time and transform from sadness and longing to precious memories and deep gratitude.

23. The Concern…Tears

Some people worry that their tears will never stop. Others think they will never be able to cry.

Consider this…

Some people believe that tears are a sign of weakness. Science tells us that tears are cleansing and healing and serve as an outlet to process and release your emotions. For those who are unable to cry, remember that tears are not mandatory.

There is no need to judge yourself. You may have been taught in childhood ideas like "men don't cry." These beliefs can block one's ability to express emotions through tears. You can find other ways to express yourself.

24. **The Concern...Moving**
For those who experience the death of their loved one at home, the need to move may surface.

Consider this...
It may be too traumatic to continue living in the house where your loved one died. There is no need to decide immediately what action to take. You can stay with a friend or family member for a few days, or even longer.

Moving to a new home can be another exhausting, unsettling experience, so postpone that decision if you can. Sometimes rearranging the room, painting it a new color, getting new furniture, etc. can bring enough change to allow you to stay in your home. Comfort can show up in unexpected ways.

25. The Concern…Purpose and meaning in life

With deep grief over the loss of a loved one, you may feel disconnected from purpose and meaning in life.

Consider this…

You may see no purpose in going on with your life without your loved one. But there is more life for you to live. Every day that passes demonstrates that you are learning to live without them. Consider this your temporary purpose.

Patience becomes your friend, even though you may not want to hear that. Meaning to your life will be restored. Time will reveal your new path and give you the energy to follow it.

Grief totally disrupts your life. I, Iris, remember being asked to speak at a Kiwanis Club meeting three months after my son's suicide. I responded that I had nothing to say. I was a failed mother. My friend responded, "My dear, you have more to say now than you ever had before." Of course, I didn't believe that, yet I am now writing my third book on grief.

May my words, with Kit Casey this time, be of service to those suffering a heart-wrenching loss and make their journey just a tiny bit easier, bringing guidance, comfort and compassion to their Spirit.

FOR FAMILIES EXPERIENCING
the COVID-19 Virus

The COVID-19 pandemic has brought suffering and deeply unsettling experiences without parallel in our time and memory. When your loved one's death is caused by this virus, expect emotions to be complicated. Due to its contagious nature and necessary preventive measures, families may not be allowed to be together during their loved one's final days. Traditional funerals or ceremonies may not be possible, delaying any chance for saying goodbye, or for closure to begin. Fear for self and other family members may amplify the complexity of your grieving.

The abrupt removal of your loved one from your life causes heartache and trauma. Unthinkable times require unusual measures, so call on your creativity and trust your instincts and heart. Find a way to plan an alternative ceremony or funeral. To do this, gather a few family members and friends together, either in person or on-line, permitting an open discussion of ideas. Listen to everyone's suggestions. Hear their needs. Make up a small guest list. Arrange for a member of the clergy to participate, if that is helpful.

Set a time and create your own service or celebration of life tribute to your loved one, even if it has to be on the Internet. Make sure your technology team rehearses and gives clear instructions to the non-techies explaining how to join in.

When you create new traditions, you are partially fulfilling the longing in your scarred heart for a more customary funeral. Choose to adjust to the loss of your burial traditions. Choose to survive your loss.

It is often recommended to do the following:

1. Write a letter to your loved one and then burn it, allowing the smoke to symbolically reach him/her to say goodbye.
2. Write a letter or letters to him/her, in gratitude for what they meant to you in life.
3. Place a photo of them in a chair and tell them how you feel. Thank them and say goodbye.

With COVID-19 and its variants, the contagion factor can cause several deaths in the same family, leading to horrific trauma for the surviving family members. Please consider professional help to assist you with this unthinkable tragedy.

Let us remember that it is through suffering that we humans meet one another, knowing no strangers. Life can regain its meaning through that kinship.

FOR FAMILIES EXPERIENCING SUICIDE
by Iris

When your loved one dies by suicide, the shock and horror can be devastating and overwhelming. I know, because my twenty-year-old son Mitch, one of four boys, ended his life on February 19, 1977. Our family was left with catastrophic trauma. Mitch was a talented musician, performer and athlete, known for being "the life of the party." His good looks and personality contributed to his popularity and the admiration of his peers.

Apparently his decision to end his life was triggered by a combination of the break up with his girlfriend, a hidden depression, feeling like a burden, and feeling trapped in never-ending emotional pain. Mitch was a good actor and able to hide his suicidal thoughts from all of us. His inability to ask for help may have been his downfall. We will never know why this was his choice. Perhaps he felt COMPELLED to end his pain in this manner.

His death came unexpectedly. We were stunned and in disbelief. One of the first questions we had was "why?" I tore at this question with fierce determination only to discover, after months and years, that there was no one cause. I found that a combination of many things contributed, allowing me to settle into some semblance of peace.

Kit and I deeply regret that you or someone you know is going through the death of a loved one by suicide. We stand beside you through our compassion and our heartfelt words. You are not alone. There are many organizations today to assist you in dealing with this loss. I have worked with all of them and have confidence they will guide you to the best of their ability.

Please consider professional help, going to a support group, or contacting any of the following organizations to find resources. Here is a list of some of the leading groups:

National Crisis Line
24 Hr.- 1-800-273-TALK (8255)

American Association of Suicidology (AAS)
www.suicidology.org

American Foundation for Suicide Prevention (AFSP)
www.afsp.org/find-support

Friends for Survival
www.friendsforsurvival.org
916-392-0664
Toll Free: (800)-646-7322

Tragedy Assistance
Program for Survivors (TAPS)
For service members, veterans and their families
www.taps.org

Part Four

———◆┼◈❀❀◈┼◆———

Self-Care Suggestions

Transformation and Possibility

"The winds of healing sift
through the windows.
Where pain and sorrow once thrived
Refreshing peace now lives.
The threads between are a tapestry of
Shared wounds and holy moments."

Iris Bolton

SELF-CARE SUGGESTIONS
After the Death of a Loved One
Concerns and Considerations

It is hard to define "self-care" because there are different perspectives on what it means. In our view, it is important to pay attention to what you want to do and what is best for you during your mourning. This is difficult, especially if you normally take care of others, putting yourself last. Even knowing what you want to do, or what is best for you, can be tough. The following is a list of suggestions for good self-care.

1. Doctor's check-up
2. Asking for help with your grief
3. Medication or not?
4. A witness for your pain
5. Decisions
6. Disagreements with friends and family
7. Setting boundaries
8. Kindness
9. Nutrition
10. Exercise
11. Meditating

12. Creativity
13. Clutter
14. Trusting your instincts
15. Laughter
16. Music
17. Vacation time and adventuring

SELF-CARE SUGGESTIONS
Concerns and Considerations

1. **The Concern... Doctor's check-up**
   Grief is exhausting and can lead to
   physical issues such as dizziness,
   upset stomach, headaches and
   even depression.

   Consider this...
   A visit to your doctor for a thorough
   checkup is a good place to start. You
   may have physical problems which
   need attention. For some, there is
   immediate comfort and relief in talking
   with their doctor and knowing someone
   is taking care of them. It provides a safe
   place to begin a conversation about your
   ailments, your stress and your grief.
   Your doctor may or may not refer you to
   a grief counselor.

2. **The Concern... Asking for help with your grief**
Some people feel they must be strong and deal with their grief by themselves. Others are comfortable asking for help.

Consider this...
Reaching out for assistance with your grief is a form of self-care. It is a strong and courageous thing to do, not a sign of weakness.

3. **The Concern...Medication or not?**
   When grief hits, you may want
   medication to take away your pain.

   Consider this...
   You are in pain. Friends and family
   may want to help you by offering their
   own medicines. Though meant well,
   unfamiliar prescription drugs can cause
   problems. If you *do* take medication, be
   sure it is only a temporary response to
   the crisis. Consult your doctor first.

4. **The Concern…A witness for your pain**
    When there is deep pain in life, most of
    us need another person to validate and
    listen to our feelings.

    Consider this…
    It is surprisingly helpful when someone
    listens to you without judgment. It helps
    you understand that your feelings are
    real and important. Find someone you
    trust and with whom you can express
    your feelings honestly.

5. **The Concern...Decisions**
   Many decisions must be made after
   someone dies. You may feel bombarded
   and rushed.

   Consider this...
   You can "decide not to decide" in
   the moment, postponing important
   decisions until you can catch your
   breath. Do not allow yourself to be
   pressured. Even though people give
   forceful advice, decisions are still yours
   to make. Speaking up and speaking
   honestly, in your own time, is a form of
   self-care.

6. **The Concern...Disagreements with friends and family**

It is common for disagreements to arise after someone dies.

Consider this...

With emotions running high, it is common for loving people to disagree. To care for yourself, you can choose not to get involved. You can walk away or say you need time to think and will talk about it later. Postponing these conversations until you feel stronger may also give time for emotions to soften and calm down.

7. **The Concern...Setting boundaries**

When grief first hits you, there may be a frenzy of people and activities around you. It can be hard to set boundaries and find balance, especially if you want to please others before yourself.

Consider this...

Be aware of your own needs. Try to find a balance between letting folks into your new world and setting limits so that you have alone time. For example, if someone asks you to go out to dinner, and you are not ready, you could respond, "Thank you for asking, I just can't do that right now."

8. **The Concern...Kindness**
Sometimes we forget to be kind to ourselves. It is easy to be gracious to others, forgetting ourselves in the process.

Consider this...
Grief gives you an opportunity to treat yourself with kindness, just as you would others. You can speak to yourself lovingly and listen closely to your needs. Follow through. Being kind to yourself may just mean saying no to someone or going to bed when you are exhausted.

9. **The Concern...Nutrition**
Nutrition is the last thing on your mind, yet many people are telling you, "You have to eat something." You may be annoyed by their insistence. You may have lost your appetite, or you may be eating junk food all day.

Consider this...
Grief is depleting. You need nutritious food to give you energy and keep you strong through this stressful time. If you have no appetite, consider drinking a meal replacement shake to give you necessary vitamins. Listen to your body and take care of it. Stay hydrated to combat fatigue.

10. **The Concern…Exercise**

In grief, some folks who have a daily exercise routine may need to keep moving. Others find that they are unable to move and tend to sit or lie down most of the day.

Consider this…

For anyone, movement is good for your body and for your well-being. Movement is a way to process your grief and release pent up emotions. Finding your own rhythm is important. Take a walk, move to music. Stretch. Just move!

11. The Concern...Meditating

Meditation (sitting and breathing) can offer you peace and calm in the whirlwind of activities that follow the death of a loved one.

Consider this...

Every day try to carve out time for you. Taking even a few minutes to meditate or sit with yourself can bring quiet and inner peace. Meditation is not for everyone, but it allows you to catch your breath and center yourself. Sitting or walking outside in nature can bring calm and can quiet the chaos in your head and heart.

12. The Concern...Creativity

After a loss, creativity seems to temporarily disappear for most of us.

Consider this...

Creativity can bring joy to your life. When you paint, bake, dance, write or play instruments, you lift your spirit. You may need to give yourself permission to create and play again, even in the midst of your pain.

I, Kit, have found painting to be a lifesaver and my therapeutic outlet. My sadness, anger and fear have been released onto the canvas.

13. The Concern...Clutter

Clutter in your home may be connected to the clutter in your mind. It may really bother you.

Consider this...

Some people need to de-clutter their home or one room just to feel they have control over something. An adrenalin surge may start a clean-up project. It may help just to be doing something. For others, the clutter may not even be noticed. Do what feels right.

14. **The Concern...Trusting your instincts**
    In times of grief, friends and family with good intentions have a need to give advice which may conflict with your ideas.

    Consider this...
    Trust your instincts. Make decisions based on what feels good and right to you. Don't let anyone overpower you with well-intended advice. Speak up or at least give yourself time to think things over. "You might feel comfortable saying, "I will think about that."

15. The Concern…Laughter

In grief, you may feel guilty just for laughing out loud. You may think you shouldn't laugh at such a terrible time. Some people fear they will never laugh again.

Consider this…
Laughter is good self-care. It can bring balance to the dark heavy emotions of grief. Laughter is healing, so welcome it. A sense of humor may also give a positive perspective on your situation.

It may surprise you if you hear yourself laugh. Enjoy the moment. Laughing during grief does not mean you love the person who died any less. It means something was funny. No guilt here!

16. The Concern…Music

Music can be helpful, quieting and comforting, yet for some people it intensifies the grief. Hearing sentimental music can bring tears or it can bring joy.

Consider this…

Again, it is your choice. Find music that suits your mood. Don't listen to music if it is too painful to hear. For many people, music can quiet your thoughts and give you some space from your grief. Be in charge of what is best for you. "Enjoy."

17. **The Concern...Vacation time and adventuring**

You may have planned and paid for a vacation in advance. What do you do?

Consider this...

A change may be good for you, but know that you will carry your grief with you; it will not stay behind. Do what feels right to you. It is probably best not to go alone. Delaying the vacation is also a consideration.

I, Iris, over the years, found that signing up for adventures was a healing distraction, and gave me revitalizing inspiration. I eventually realized how short life is and that I wanted to risk doing something really fun and outside my norm. I swam with 300 dolphins in the wild in Hawaii. I climbed Machu Pichu in Peru. I started studying with Oscar Miro-Quesada, a Peruvian shamanic teacher and healer, and became an apprentice. These and other adventures helped to heal my soul.

There are many other forms of self-care. It can be extremely useful to provide respite from your pain through nourishing, bite-sized diversions. This might look like an herb scented soak in the tub, a movie night with popcorn, listening to a podcast by your favorite commentator, taking a relaxing massage or simply hanging out with your animal friends. And, honestly, a walk in nature cures much of what ails us all.

Each person's personality and needs will express differently. Just remember to honor the time and passage of pain and grief that exists for you right now.

Part Five

Finding Support

Hope and Healing

"Grief can feel like you're under a weighted blanket, blocking out light & hope, and making it hard to breathe. But time is a gift, and one day you'll find you have the strength to slide out from under its weight, and move, dance even, squinting at the light with a strange new optimism.

Tomorrow you may find yourself back under grief's weight, but you now know that freedom is possible."

Kit Casey

FINDING SUPPORT
After the Death of a Loved One

It is difficult to grieve alone and it is not necessary. There are support groups in many churches and synagogues and the Internet is full of helpful organizations and resources. Check out their legitimacy before you commit to them. The following is a list of options to consider as you search for guidance and support:

1. Asking for help
2. Counseling
3. Talking out loud with the person who died
4. Resources (support groups, books, on-line assistance)
5. Journaling
6. Tasks of grief
7. Psychics, mediums and intuitive counselors
8. Metaphysical events / Visitations / Mystical happenings
9. Rituals and habits
10. Your faith or spirituality

FINDING SUPPORT SUGGESTIONS
For Consideration

1. **Asking for help**

   Consider this...
   Asking for help with your grief may be
   the most important thing you can do
   for yourself. You may feel it is a sign of
   weakness, when actually it is a sign of
   strength. Before sharing, ensure you are
   with people with whom you feel safe.

2. **Counseling**

Consider this...
Speaking to a professional grief
counselor is always an option. You may
receive insights and skills to deal with
the complex emotions of grief. It can be
a safe place to share intimate feelings
without judgment.

3. **Talking out loud to the person who died**

Consider this...

Talking to your loved one out loud, after their death, may seem bizarre but can bring you comfort and support. It provides an outlet for your emotions and a way to talk through unresolved issues. It can help you still feel connected to them.

4. **Resources (support groups, books, on-line assistance)**

   Consider this...
   Finding resources such as support groups, books, on-line assistance etc. can be difficult, especially when you are low on energy, due to your grief. Many organizations, such as the following, have been established to assist you.

Mental Health America- 703-684-7722
www.mentalhealthamerica.net

Compassionate Friends- 877-969-0010
www.compassionatefriends.org

**The National Center for Grieving Children
& Families
The Dougy Center- 503.775.5683**
www.dougy.org/grief-support-resources

**Hospice Foundation of America-
800-854-3402**
www.hospicefoundation.org

5. **Journaling**

Consider this...
Writing about your feelings in a journal may be not be right for everyone. You may not have the energy for it. Some people love the idea. It is an outlet for their emotions and keeps a record of their progress. It is a way of clearing your head and sometimes gives you answers to your own questions.

We have known people who keep a gratitude journal to find a balance to their pain.

6. **Tasks of grief**

Consider this…
A woman, whose name we don't know, stood up at a conference and shared her prescription for mourning. Her guidelines have become a mantra for many of us.
1) Tell the story of what happened; it will help you believe the truth of it.
2) Express all emotions, (guilt, anger, shame, etc.) by writing, talking screaming, wailing, punching pillows.
3) Transition from the physical presence of your loved one to another kind of relationship, such as through a spiritual connection or through your dreams.
4) In time, make meaning out of the tragedy. Birthing something positive from the trauma can make a difference in your life. In turn, when you help others in their grief, it uplifts each of your lives.

7. **Psychics, mediums and intuitive counselors**

Consider this…
Out of curiosity you may consider seeing a psychic, a medium or a counselor with intuitive skills. This is not for everyone, yet it may have some benefits in your search for answers. Be discerning. Use only what is useful.

8. **Metaphysical events / Visitations / Mystical happenings**

Consider this...

As you grieve, mysterious and unexplained phenomenon may occur. They can come through dreams, visitations and signs which you may believe came from your loved one. You may find a feather, a penny, or some kind of comforting sign. If you don't believe in any of this, just let it go.

9.   **Rituals / Habits**

Consider this...
A ritual is an observance which may
give you balance and continuity in your
life. For example, it may be as simple
as making your bed every morning
as you think of them, or touching a
photograph of your loved one when
leaving the room, or going to the grave
site regularly. It is a positive, conscious
action reminding you of your loved one.
It may be empowering, or it may be of
no interest to you.

10. **Your faith or spirituality can bring you comfort and support**

   Consider this...
   Your trust in God or in your faith may be a strong support for you. Your spirituality may be your guide. Leaning on whatever gives you strength and peace is the important thing. If you are an atheist, look for other comforting sources to sustain you.

A Closing on Acceptance

As we look at closing this little book on grief, the topic of acceptance in the presence of loss surfaces as a critical next step. From personal experience, we recognize that this stage of grief cannot be rushed and is also essential. We wondered, as authors of this work: "How can we speak to the considerations and suggestions guiding us to the ultimate soul of the book…acceptance and gratitude?"

The answer came in part from our friend, Robin Harman, editor and teacher. She shared a story from Buddhist literature that illustrates the pain, struggle and eventual inner resolution of sorrow.

"In essence the tale speaks of a young mother whose excruciating pain upon the death of her infant son leads her to reach out to her community…only to realize, in due course, that *everyone, everywhere*, has experienced death and suffering. With time and in listening to other's stories, she comes to understand the universality of loss, and finds peace in the face of bereavement. Only then can she let go of her young son.

In early stages, as we move toward acceptance, words fail. Yet words are largely what we have, as humans, to express our unimaginable sorrow and speak of the seemingly unbearable hole in our hearts. We may feel that joy will never again brighten our lives, and see our grief expanded and mirrored in one another's eyes. That is one reality.

Heavy hearts also hold profound portions of love within them. The connective tissue of *shared* pain creates a compassionate web of sustenance that prepares us for each step through the fog. Each clear-eyed moment of choice to feel and absorb this *new* reality moves us toward acceptance.

The nature of love tells us that those you have loved *always* serve to "grow" your heart, even when wounded. Eventually this brokenness can become whole, and awaken you to new perceptions. With a willingness to remain open, previously painful memories can mysteriously elicit remembrances of unfathomable love. The bittersweet pain of loss can gradually fade*."

May this terrible journey of grief bring each of us closer to one another, born of shared empathy of experience. It is our hope and prayer that plumbing these depths creates an opening for you to a re-discovered purpose and enhanced acceptance of the ultimate possibility and beauty of life beyond grief.

---

* Robin Harman

Epilogue
Thoughts on Gratitude
by Kit

Gratitude is one of those flowery obscure overused words, like love or forgiveness, that you don't really want to hear when you're immersed in the pain of grief. But just like love and forgiveness, it has power. Very simply, it has power to calm your body and hush your pain in the second it takes to be thankful for ANYTHING (a memory, the sunshine, a clean pair of socks). That hush may be fleeting, but it is real and makes a difference in every cell in your body.

There are a lot of things, like death and dying, where we're not in control, but living in gratitude is something we can choose to control. It gives our pain a break, if only for a moment. It makes everything within that moment good and perfect and meant to be. It lets us rest.

Living in a *constant* state of gratitude is a superhuman feat, and superhuman I am *not*. I have to remind myself multiple times a day to look around and name something or someone for which I'm grateful. Yet the pain of grief quiets when I do. A simple thank you to the Universe is like opening a window and breathing in fresh air. Even a few times a day is enough to make a difference. As my gratitude muscle grows, my sorrow fades.

Regardless of the cause of death of your loved one, there can come a time, beyond the chaos of those stubborn emotions (sadness, loneliness, regret) when gratitude overpowers heartache: gratitude for time spent together, memories made (good and bad), food you enjoyed, tv shows you watched, their perfect weaknesses, the love you shared, their laugh.

Thinking thankfully of moments in the past with your loved one, and moments now still touched by them, it becomes possible to realize how blessed we *were* with them, how blessed we *are* now because of them, and how beautiful and precious the gift of life *is*, always.

Dear Friend,

We believe the difficult experience of bereavement can be transformative. It will change your life. Trust your own instincts as to the healing path you will take. If, in this moment, it is difficult to believe you will survive, be patient. Ultimately you will find in yourself the belief that your intention to survive this loss will manifest in your life, for yourself, your family and your friends.

We believe that where your wound is lays the promise and potential for your own personal healing and hope. Know you are not alone. Your grief is unique. Grief takes many forms. Judge not. Give yourself permission to ask for help when needed. Know that your loved one will always be remembered as you carry their memory in your heart.

May the words in this little book bring you thoughts and feelings to help you through the dark days and bring you into brighter

135

times. We are sorry for your loss. We trust that if you have questions, not addressed here, you will continue your search. There may be no definitive answers, yet you can live with hunches, guesses, and your own instincts. May they bring you peace.

In grief we meet no strangers. In friendship we offer our "considerations" with compassion for your broken heart and for your resiliency and your healing power.

As you continue your healing and your journey of mourning, consider writing your own story. It is a therapeutic way of honestly sharing and assisting others as it helps you process your own feelings. Remember to be kind to yourself and to create a support system around you. Your experience of loss creates unique possibilities for you to make a difference in the world.

In time, you will be able to move from torment to wounded healer, giving meaning to the life of your loved one. Your survival will be a testimony to the courage and resilience of the human spirit.

Blessings and love,

Chris and *Kit*

Part Six

Acknowledgments

Acceptance and Gratitude

"What brings peace and solitude above all is
Acceptance of the What Is.
Gratitude for the tough lessons.
Finding the resiliency within and living it.
Balancing reasonableness with passion and
being alive with purpose.
Someone/something to love and
Grace to tie it all up in one package.
This I know. This all is Holy."

Lynn Namke

ACKNOWLEDGMENTS

The Little Book on Grief
Concerns to Consider

Dedication from Iris:

To Kit Casey, my cherished niece, co-author and artist. Your gentle soul and tender heart enhance this book with your gifts of humor, depth of compassion and insight, and your inspiring sacred art. You are a bright light in the world.

To my beloved husband Jack Bolton for providing me a foundation for my work and for years of loving support. Your cheer leading, kindness and listening skills have kept me grounded and creative. Blessings my love!

To our son, Bill Bolton, whose technical expertise has been life saving. Almost daily you have taught me to deal with the mischief of the computer with patience. Your sensitivity and wise reflections profoundly impact this book.

To Robin Harman, friend and believer in miracles. Your gift of editing skills, and your ability to touch our book with your special magic and wisdom, is a talent unsurpassed.

To sons John and Bobby and to our entire family, no words can express the gratitude I feel for your sustaining love and encouragement. You nourish my soul.

To our Mitch, whose devastating decision to give up on life, started a landslide awareness of the universal problem of death by suicide in the United States. May you know that your search for answers has spread around the world and has led to our own pursuit, understanding and ability to help others.

Dedication from Kit:

To my beautiful children, Ben and Sarah, whose love and light teach me every day what real strength is. Thank you for making me laugh.

To Aunt Iris, for allowing me to grieve openly on paper...a therapeutic venture in itself (but you knew that, didn't you?) that opened the door to acceptance and that elusive little thing called gratitude, for what was and what is. Thank you, Aunt Iris. You are a gift.

To Dad, Dave, Tibby, Tori, Jim and "All Those People." How blessed we are!

And to Mom and Steve, the brightest stars in the night sky. Always missing you.

Copyright 2021 by Iris Bolton and Kit Casey
The Little Book on Grief..... ISBN 978-1-928723-01-1
First Printing ....March 27, 2021
Co-Authors: Iris Bolton and Kit Casey

Artwork: Kit Casey
Technical Advisor: Bill Bolton
Designing Editor: Robin Harman
Production Manager: Madelyn Spiegelman
Pre-Press/Designer: Candace Petron
First Editor: Jack Bolton
Proof Reading Team:
    Robin Harman
    Cynthia Lind
    Debbie Loshbough
    Diane Rhea
    Jandee Walker
Publisher: Bolton Press Atlanta
Printer: BookLogix

For information:
Visit: www.IrisBolton.com
Email: Orders@IrisBolton.com
Call: 770-645-1886

ABOUT THE AUTHORS

Iris Bolton is a counselor, author and Director Emeritus of The Link Counseling Center in Atlanta, GA. She served as Director of this non-profit center for twenty-six years. In l977, Iris and her husband were devastated by the suicide of their 20-year-old son, Mitch. She looked for something to read to give them guidance. She found nothing. A few years later her sister, age 65, died of cancer. Then her mother and father died of natural causes at ninety-five years of age, two years apart.

After several years of mourning, Iris wrote the book "My Son...My Son...A Guide to Healing after Death, Loss or Suicide," pioneering the suicide aftercare movement in the United States. More recently she authored "Voices of Healing and Hope; Conversations on Grief after Suicide," highlighting the stories of at least thirty-five suicide loss survivors. The DVD is available on-line at www.IrisBolton.com/Interviews.

Kit Casey, Iris's beloved niece, is an artist and mother of two children. After attending Southern Methodist University in Dallas, TX, she graduated from The American College for the Applied Arts in Atlanta, GA. Kit worked as a graphic artist in Birmingham, AL, and continued that career in Boston, MA, where she and her husband also owned and operated a business. Currently she runs the Kit Casey Studio in Boston. (kitcaseystudio.com)

In 2019, Kit's mother died of natural causes at the age of ninety-four. Three months later Kit's husband died of cancer. Iris knew that her niece had children to care for and a business to run. With little time to read and no ability to concentrate, Kit needed an easy-to-navigate guide to mourning. Iris resolved to write a little book on common concerns faced during grief, and she believed that the sharing of two women about their losses, both long ago and recent, could help others.

After the one-year anniversary of the death of Kit's mother and husband, the two women decided to collaborate and co-author this book. The powerfully creative and abstract artwork is the creation of Kit Casey.

Iris Bolton

Kit Casey

Other Books by Iris

My tendency, laughed at teasingly by friends, has been to give away as many copies of my books as possible. My desire has been to increase outreach in support of healing in the presence of grief and loss.

My commitment with this little book is to make it available, free, to anyone and everyone who can be served by its contents.

With that in mind, if you have interest in supporting my heart's desire, an opportunity to pay it forward is offered here. Note than all funds will go directly, and solely, to cover printing and handling costs of The Little Book.

> Visit: www.IrisBolton.com
> Email: Orders@IrisBolton.com
> Phone: 770-645-1886

Testimonials

"Each person is in your life for a reason, a season, or a lifetime. The Little Book on Grief is an essential user's guide to love, loss and living. No need to find right words to say, just "Here is a little book to ease your way."

> *Dwana M. Bush,* MD
> Family Physician
> Hospice and Palliative Care

"Iris and Kit have captured a world of concerns in this Little Book. Between the pages are art, humanity, cautions and concerns that anyone attempting the grief journey will want to visit over and over along the way. Iris Bolton continues to teach and provide guidance for those thrown into the troubled waters of sudden and traumatic loss. Kit Casey inspires us with the beauty and honesty of her work. The ability to paint pain and hope is not one many have the capacity to do unless they have had both.

Tips and beauty are not as easily found in grief without such a guidebook and both are contained inside this one…a book you read and return to, perhaps mark sections, and share with others you meet on your pathway to healing."

Frank R. Campbell Ph.D, LCSW, C.T.
Executive Director Emeritus,
Baton Rouge Crisis Intervention

"My beloved sister Iris Bolton has once again provided a dose of exquisite heart medicine for our world. In collaboration with her niece Kit Casey, her latest wisdom offering on how to navigate the challenges that come with the loss of a loved one, entitled The Little Book on Grief: Concerns to Consider, is a true healing salve for our human soul. Not only do they plant extremely heart-nurturing seeds of awareness within the experiential field of their readers, they, likewise, offer a series of clear and concise soul teachings to help transform the pain of loss into an opening for growth, restoring wholeness to their lives. Thank you, Iris and Kit!"

don Oscar Miro-Quesada, founder
The Heart of the Healer
www.theheartofthehealer.org

Index

"In the midst of winter, I found there
was, within me, an invincible summer."

Albert Camus

Resilience and Renewal
Red rose, as memory held in your heart.
Dream your future...

159